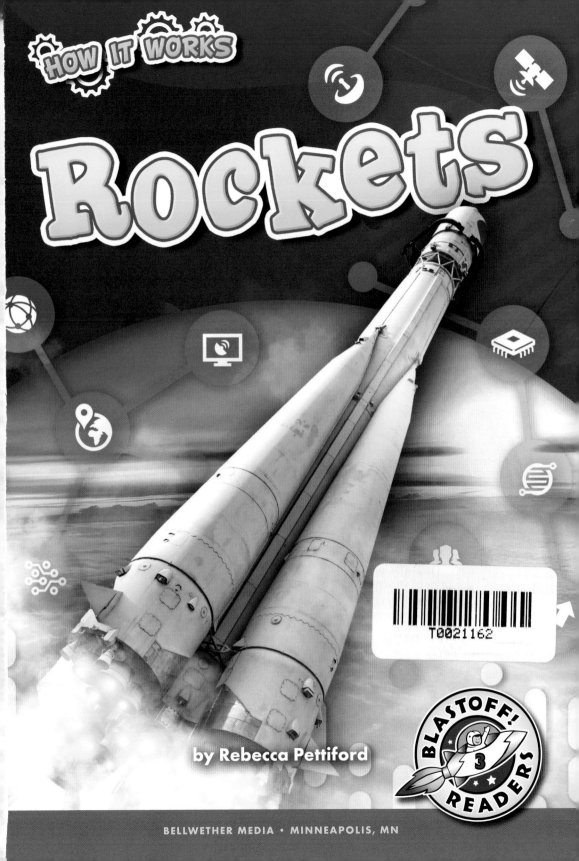

HOW IT WORKS

Rockets

by Rebecca Pettiford

T0021162

BLASTOFF! READERS
3

BELLWETHER MEDIA • MINNEAPOLIS, MN

Blastoff! Readers are carefully developed by literacy experts to build reading stamina and move students toward fluency by combining standards-based content with developmentally appropriate text.

Level 1 provides the most support through repetition of high-frequency words, light text, predictable sentence patterns, and strong visual support.

Level 2 offers early readers a bit more challenge through varied sentences, increased text load, and text-supportive special features.

Level 3 advances early-fluent readers toward fluency through increased text load, less reliance on photos, advancing concepts, longer sentences, and more complex special features.

★ **Blastoff! Universe**

Reading Level

BLASTOFF! Beginners — Grade **K**

BLASTOFF! READERS — Grades **1–3**

BLASTOFF! DISCOVERY — Grade **4**

This edition first published in 2022 by Bellwether Media, Inc.

No part of this publication may be reproduced in whole or in part without written permission of the publisher. For information regarding permission, write to Bellwether Media, Inc., Attention: Permissions Department, 6012 Blue Circle Drive, Minnetonka, MN 55343.

Library of Congress Cataloging-in-Publication Data

Names: Pettiford, Rebecca, author.
Title: Rockets / by Rebecca Pettiford.
Description: Minneapolis, MN : Bellwether Media, Inc., 2022. | Series: Blastoff! Readers: How it works | Includes bibliographical references and index. | Audience: Ages 5-8 | Audience: Grades 2-3 | Summary: "Simple text and full-color photography introduce beginning readers to how rockets work. Developed by literacy experts for students in kindergarten through third grade"-- Provided by publisher.
Identifiers: LCCN 2021049244 (print) | LCCN 2021049245 (ebook) | ISBN 9781644876015 (library binding) | ISBN 9781648346767 (paperback) | ISBN 9781648346125 (ebook)
Subjects: LCSH: Rockets (Aeronautics)--Juvenile literature. | CYAC: Rockets (Aeronautics)
Classification: LCC TL782.5 .P455 2022 (print) | LCC TL782.5 (ebook) | DDC 621.43/56--dc23/eng/20211103
LC record available at https://lccn.loc.gov/2021049244
LC ebook record available at https://lccn.loc.gov/2021049245

Text copyright © 2022 by Bellwether Media, Inc. BLASTOFF! READERS and associated logos are trademarks and/or registered trademarks of Bellwether Media, Inc.

Editor: Betsy Rathburn   Series Design: Jeffrey Kollock   Book Designer: Gabriel Hilger

Printed in the United States of America, North Mankato, MN.

Table of Contents

What Are Rockets?

Rockets are powerful machines. They carry **astronauts** to space. They also carry **satellites** and other spacecraft.

Rockets help scientists study Earth and space.

satellite

space shuttle *Atlantis*

5

How Do Rockets Work?

All rockets have a **structural system**. This is the main body. It holds the rocket's parts together.

The **payload** is what rockets carry. Rockets need a lot of power to **launch** heavy loads.

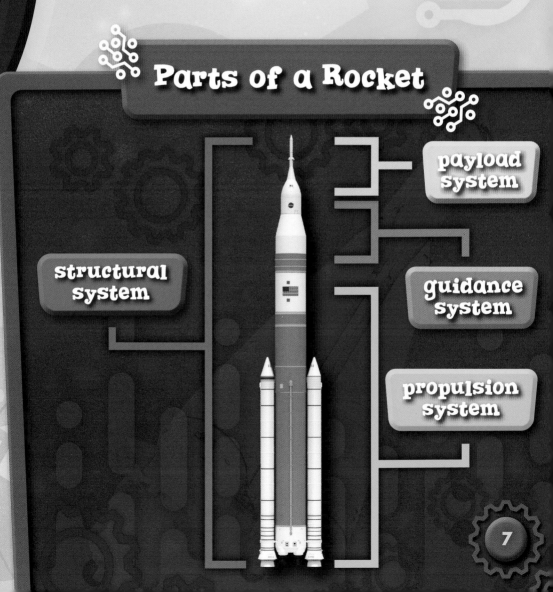

Parts of a Rocket

payload system

structural system

guidance system

propulsion system

The **guidance system** helps rockets find their way. It uses computers.

Atlas V 541
rocket

It helps rockets get to space safely. It keeps them **stable**. It controls their movements.

rocket
engines

The **propulsion system** holds the engine. It is what makes rockets launch.

The rocket's fuel mixes with **oxygen** in the engine. This creates a strong blast. The blast pushes out **exhaust**.

fuel tank

exhaust

Exhaust flows down from the bottom of the rocket. Exhaust is very hot, and it moves very fast.

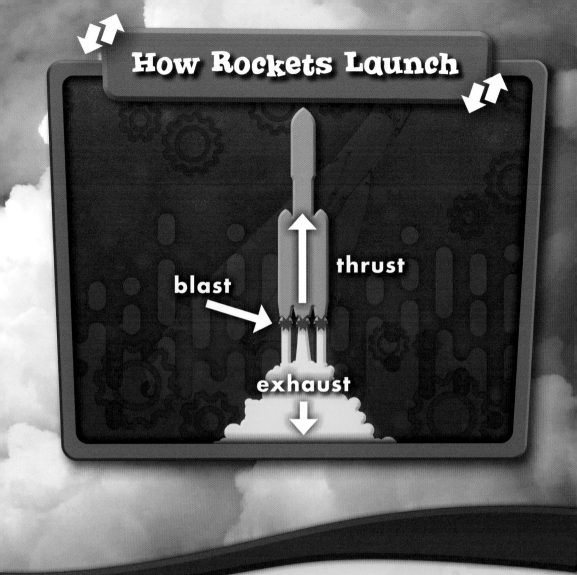

How Rockets Launch

thrust

blast

exhaust

Exhaust creates **thrust**. Thrust pushes the rocket up. The rocket launches into the air!

One blast is not enough to reach space. **Staging** helps rockets go farther. As a rocket goes higher, it breaks into smaller rockets.

These are called stages. Each rocket has two or three stages.

stage after breaking off of a rocket

staging

Stages have their own engines.
They supply extra thrust.
The stages fall back to Earth
as they run out of fuel.

Staging

1 launch

2 stage 1

3 stage 2

payload

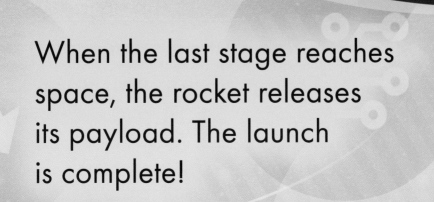

When the last stage reaches
space, the rocket releases
its payload. The launch
is complete!

The Future of Rockets

Today's rockets easily reach space. They launch spacecraft and bring astronauts to space. They have even helped astronauts reach the moon!

But scientists want to go farther. They must build more powerful rockets.

Nuclear rockets may come next. They will be 100 times faster than rockets today!

What do you think future rockets will be able to do?

Faster rockets could help astronauts travel farther into space. One day, astronauts may use a rocket to get to Mars!

Glossary

astronauts—people who are trained to travel in a spacecraft

exhaust—a mixture of gases that is released by machines that burn fuel

guidance system—the system that keeps the rocket stable and controls its movements

launch—to send or shoot something into space

nuclear rockets—rockets that are powered by the heat from a nuclear reaction

oxygen—one of the gases that make up the air

payload—the things a rocket carries into space, such as people or spacecraft

propulsion system—the system responsible for the force that moves the rocket forward; the propulsion system holds a rocket's engine and fuel.

satellites—spacecraft that move around a planet, the sun, or the moon

stable—not easily changed or likely to change

staging—the process of launching a rocket with two or three stages; each stage starts connected and breaks off when it runs out of fuel.

structural system—the body of a rocket

thrust—the force that pushes something forward

To Learn More

AT THE LIBRARY

Borgert-Spaniol, Megan. *Create a Rocket! and More Flight Challenges*. Minneapolis, Minn.: Abdo Publishing, 2021.

McAnulty, Stacy. *Mars! Earthlings Welcome*. New York, N.Y.: Henry Holt and Co., 2021.

Murray, Julie. *Satellites*. Minneapolis, Minn.: Abdo Zoom, 2020.

ON THE WEB

FACTSURFER

Factsurfer.com gives you a safe, fun way to find more information.

1. Go to www.factsurfer.com.

2. Enter "rockets" into the search box and click 🔍.

3. Select your book cover to see a list of related content.

Index

The images in this book are reproduced through the courtesy of: Igor Bukhlin, front cover; Dima Zel, pp. 3, 4 (satellite); NPeter, p. 4 (Earth); Bill Ingalls/ NASA, pp. 4-5; NASA Archive/ Alamy, pp. 6-7; Terry White/ SLS/ NASA, pp. 7, 17, 19; SpaceX/ NASA, pp. 8-9; Tony Gray and Tim Powers/ NASA, p. 9; Mia2you, pp. 10-11; NASA, pp. 11, 14 (inset), 14-15; Artsiom R., pp. 12-13; JWM/ NASA/ LANDSAT/ Alamy, pp. 18-19; Geopix/ Alamy, pp. 20-21;